FATHER TO SON

Mason,
Reach for the stars!

-BYJW 23'

WRITTEN BY: KENJI L. JACKSON

WITH: HEDDRICK MCBRIDE

ILLUSTRATED BY: HH-PAX

EDITED BY: JILL MCKELLAN

ISBN-10:1492710148

ISBN-13:978-1492710141

DEDICATION

This book is dedicated to all parents who understand that being a parent is a full time commitment; ensuring that you are doing everything possible to provide your children with the tools needed to build a bright future. The *Father to Son* series is inspired by my son, Kaiden Li, who has brought happiness to my life everyday and pushes me to be the best father I can be.

I want to thank my parents, family, and closest friends. I thank the men of Tenacious, Talented, and Capable and Morgan State University; as well as Nile Style Barber Shop for your unwavering love and support.

LOVE YOUR MOTHER

Love and honor your mother because you only get one.

She will love you no matter what because you are her son.

Your mother will teach you important things
you need to know.

She will get you ready for life
and help you grow.

But also son, take care of your mother and give her a hand.

Help out around the house as much as you can.

Respect your mother
and follow her rules.
Conduct yourself properly
at home and in school.

Work really hard
and make your mother proud.
Be a leader, not a follower.
Stand out from the crowd.

Show your mother you are responsible
and see the joy it brings.
Be reliable, trustworthy,
and do the little things.

Tell your mother you love her when you kiss
and hold her tight.
Make her life easier
and always treat her right.

These are some things
that will make your mother smile.
She will be proud to have a son
who goes the extra mile.

EDUCATION

A good education is one of the keys to success.

Use what you learn and try to do your best.

Once you have an education no one can take it away.

However, you still need to try to learn new things each day.

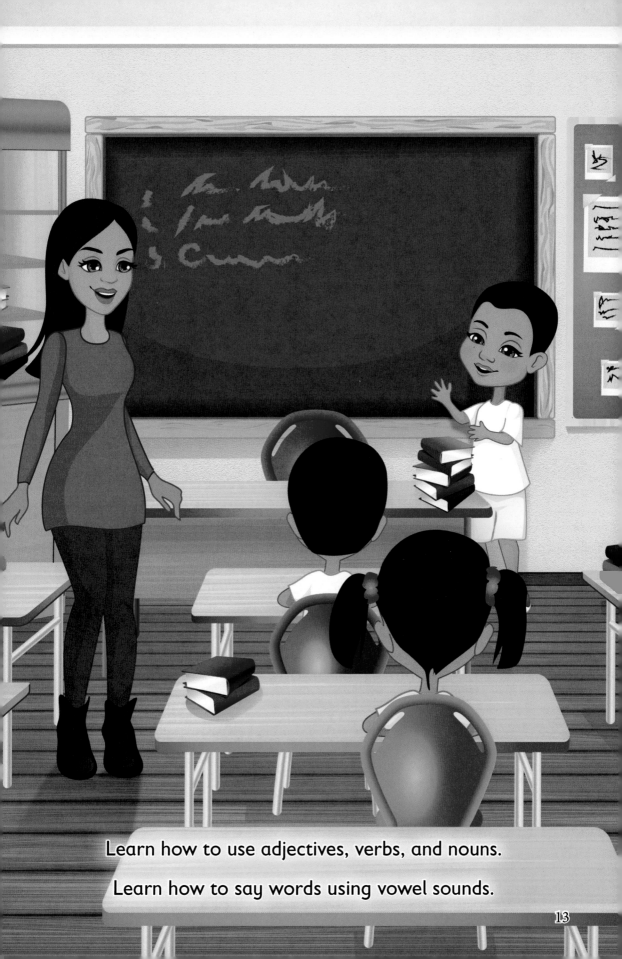

Learn how to use adjectives, verbs, and nouns.

Learn how to say words using vowel sounds.

13

Practice writing neatly and check for mistakes
before you're done.
You may need writing to do your job
or you can do it for fun.

In science, learn biology,
about the elements, and their icons.
Learn chemistry, mass and matter,
protons and neutrons.

Math is very important
and we use it day and night.
For example, it's used when telling time,
using money, and measuring weight and height.

Knowing history and a second language
can help you to really soar.
Having different skills and being educated
can open many a door.

You will go to elementary, middle,
high school, and college;
Every step of the way you
will gain more knowledge.

You can be a doctor, lawyer,
own a business, or fix cars.
Having a good education allows you
to reach for the stars.

The more you know the more options you will have.

A good education helps keep you on the right path.

15

RESPECT

Respect should be given and respect should be received.
Respect is an important value, which every child needs.

Respect your parents, relatives, friends, and adults.
Respect for each other produces positive results.

You must respect your mother,
women, and girls too.
Respect people in your neighborhood
and your teachers in school.

Respect people's space
and make sure they respect yours too.
Respect the good in others
and the good things they do.

If someone is talking to you,
show respect and listen.
You may learn something new
you were previously missing.

Use respectful language
and do not call people names.
Keep your hands to yourself
and have others do the same.

If you have a problem,
express yourself with respect.
Try not to be mean
and say things you may regret.

Respect those around you
even when you have a bad day.
Being respectful to others
can go a long way.

Whether in the gym or on the field,

at home or in school;

Being a part of a team

that works together can be really cool.

There is no "I" in team; it's never just about you.
Yet your actions, good or bad, will affect how you all do.

Help a teammate in need and strive to get along.
Everyone working together is what makes the team strong.

At home everyone does their job
to keep the house clean.
Clean up behind yourself
and do chores to help the home team.

In school you and your classmates
are there to learn and grow.
Pay attention, do your work,
and show what you know.

On the field or on the court,
work hard and do your part.
Listen to your coaches
and lead by example from the start.

Losing can be hard
and winning feels great.
Whether you win or lose, be a good sport
and a positive teammate.

Never give up, stick together,
and stand tall.
No matter what team you're a part of,
have fun and give your all.

MANNERS

Show you have manners. Be courteous and polite.
If you are going to try something, try doing it right.

Take pride in how you look and in the things you say.
Make your parents proud by carrying yourself the right way.

When talking to someone
always make eye contact.
Speak with confidence
and think before you react.

Say thank you or no thank you,
you're welcome and please.
Say excuse me to people
whenever you sneeze.

Comb and brush your hair
and remember to brush your teeth.
When getting dressed,
make sure your clothes are neat.

Always cover your mouth
when you cough or yawn.
After all, germs stay in the air
even after you are gone.

While in a public place,
use your inside voice.
Speaking calmly instead of yelling
is always a good choice.

Stand strong when you walk
and be proud of who you are.
How you carry yourself and the manners
you have can take you very far.

VISIT
WWW.MCBRIDESTORIES.COM
FOR MORE TITLES

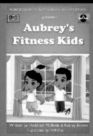

Made in the USA
Middletown, DE
02 May 2023

29751728R00020